Inspirational Ducks

Nick Pinfield

Illustrated by Caroline Holden

Chalgrove Press

A CIP catalogue record for this book is available from the British Library

ISBN   0-9547539-1-7

Designed by Alan Chaston
Printed and bound by Alden, Oxford

Published by:
Chalgrove Press
The Old Vicarage
97 High Street
Chalgrove, Oxford
OX44 7SS   UK

Dedication

To ducks everywhere. May you dabble contentedly on the Great Pond of Life.

'Like Sisyphus, our work is never done;
Continually rolls back the restless stone'

Stephen Duck,
The Thresher's Labour 1730

Contents

Britducks

Queen Bouduckea

A fierce warrior chieftain from East Anglia, this pugnacious duck led the Iceni in revolt against the occupying Roman army (no Essex-girl white stiletto jokes here please. Ed). She has become for this reason something of a national icon, with a statue on the Embankment near Westminster Bridge demonstrating fine chariot driving technique. No doubt she was described as a terrorist by Pompous Moronus, the Roman military Governor of Britannia at the time.

Frustrated motorists stuck in the inevitable traffic jams in Whitehall and Parliament Square could do worse than fit sharp scythes to the wheels of their Nissans. They would scratch a lot of cars and decapitate short and unwary tourists but get home to Ongar in record time.

Dick the Duck Nurdler

Duck nurdling is, in these automated farm-factory days, a lost rural skill. In former times every village of any size boasted a duck nurdler as well as a blacksmith, cobbler and butcher. The lost art of nurdling was passed down the generations, jealously guarded by the Guild of Duck Nurdlers. All that remains is a group of over-fed city types who gather at regular intervals in their splendid duck-shaped dining hall in Poultrey to celebrate a skill of which they know nothing and care less.

Richard of Duckington, Cheshire, was one of the pilgrims riding to Canterbury in the 1380s. 'The Duck Nurdler's Tale' has rather mysteriously been deleted from current versions of Chaucer's Canterbury Tales but can be found in the first printed version by Caxton a century or so later. Indeed, so well established was the craft, that among Caxton's first titles is 'Teach Yourself Duck Nurdling' (1487).

Mary Shelduck

Who would have thought that this demure and proper 19th century duck would have given birth to one of the scariest literary creations of the age – Frankenduck, half man, half monster, half duck. Perhaps it is not so surprising, for beneath the starched respectability of middle class ducks such as she, often seethed an excess of Byronic Romanticism.

Her brother Percy , the celebrated poet, had most of the fun. He even died tragically young, swamped and drowned while paddling off the coast of Italy by a passing ocean liner or possibly Moby Duck far from home. *Ode to a Mallard* by Percy Bysshe Shelduck is rightly considered a poetic gem (O Wild West Duck, thou breath of par-boiled cabbage....etc)

Duck Whittington

London can be a cruel place. The festering alleys and crumbling tenements of the medieval capital city were as slow as their modern, slightly more salubrious, counterparts to acknowledge self-evident talent. Evident to Duck. And his Mum. And his cat.

Turned down for the umpteenth time in his application as a Traffic Warden, he decided to leave the ungrateful city with his cat and seek his fortune elsewhere. Waddling through Highgate away from London, they bumped into yet another drab, dawdling bird, evidently lost. 'Ruddy tourists' muttered Duck. 'No' replied his talkative moggy 'Tern again'. Duck misheard. Turned. Became Traffic Warden then Lord Mayor. Many panto performances. Congestion charges. Lord Duck of Brent.

Duck Turpin

"Stand and Deliver !". These words sent a chill of fear through the travelling ducks of old. They wore masks, these gentleducks of the road but nothing could disguise the jutting beak, rasping croak and rancid breath of the notorious Duck Turpin.

It was not always so. An expensive education at the exclusive Downside had equipped him with little more than the ability to say hooray to Henry. Limited even by the modest abilities of his peers, he found employment with The Feather Truck Company . Came the day he arrived late with a package to find the assignee trundling off down the lane. "Stand. I'm delivering !" he quacked. This was misunderstood. Pursued by an angry mob he fled to become the legendary DT. The privations of a life on the road were as nothing compared to the casual brutalities of Downside. He thrived. He prospered. He had saved enough to send his son to the old school before he was caught, tried and transported for life to the Colonies.

Lord Lover Duck

Never was Hegel's dictum that 'The owl of Minerva paints grey on grey' better exemplified than by Harold Duck's twenty years in the House as Member of Parliament for Erewhon South. At the end of that time, nobody had ever heard of him. He had gloriously failed to make a single speech, ask a single question or so much as feature in Hansard for a meaningful eyebrow twitch. For this outstanding service to his Party, Harold was elevated to the Upper House.

When the new Noble Lord was asked to declare his choice of title, a minor setback occurred. About to mutter 'Lord Greyduck of Obscurity', a passing cockney Pearly King (actually a redundant stockbroker from Farnham) declaimed 'Lawd Luvver Duck' for the benefit of a party of tourists he was escorting beside the Mother of Parliaments. Characteristically, this least amorous of ducks bore his misfortune with a certain meek resignation. Some even detected a faintly jaunty swagger.

Duck Bill Platypus

Distantly related to Cyrano de Bergerac, Bill's ancestors specialised in petty larceny, muggings and occasional membership of Uncle Duck Turpin's Highway Crew (see above or below or somewhere). Short legs and a massive conk did not lend themselves to the quick getaway and evasion needed to escape even the lethargic forces of law and order. Caught, tried and sentenced to penal servitude in the colonies, the Platypus family carved out a niche in the young and dynamic society of Australia.

Bill's upward social mobility was much assisted by his scornful denunciations of Whingeing Poms – a prerequisite for the aspiring Australian politiduck. A master of the blindingly obvious remark, his tiresome, derivative and oft-repeated observations achieved a certain celebrity, becoming known as 'Platitudes'. As Sir William Platypus he became a national symbol and features on coins, stamps etc.

SIR WILLIAM PLATYPUS

The Duckess of Argyll

Perhaps you need to be of a certain age to recall the notoriety of this aristocratic duck. Inventive in pursuit of her particular interests, she brought a whiff of sulphur to the placid lochs and glens of Argyll.

To the undisguised delight of the tabloid press, her exploits sold newspapers for months. Such lurid tales enlivened many a journey on the Central Line back to Ongar. There is perhaps more understanding today for the frustrations of a spirited duck marooned in a gloomy Highland castle. Can we now forgive her kilted canoodlings ? Ask the Duck of Argyll.

Dixon of Duck Green

Ah me. Warm beer, village cricket, social deference, Dan Dare. Those were the days. You could leave your house unlocked, secure in the knowledge that the few malefactors abroad would be caught in the act, cuffed and escorted to the local nick by PC George Dixon. Evenin' all. Or so we were led to believe by the flickering black and white postage stamp that was the television screen on the large box sitting in the front room beneath the flying ducks.

Duck Green was the community we all hoped we were inhabiting. It was as bogus as all these televisual inventions, of course, but a lot more reassuring than Sun Hill or South Los Angeles.

Duck Bogarde

Born Eric Crunge in Acton in 1926, his latent career in the embryonic British postwar film industry stuttered through bit parts in Ealing Comedies and bite parts in third rate vampire movies. The occasional codpiece role in early Carry On films was scant compensation. He changed his name to Duck Bogarde, affecting a languid but intense continental swagger. His future was assured. His dashing young medical student in Ducktor in the House caused a flutter in many a starched blouse.

His journey from Darling of the Odeons through mittel european aristocrat to troubled recluse is well known. No Hollywood vulgarity here. More Acton angst.

The Surrey Ducks

There is no doubt that this famous family is not what it was. Always somewhat in the shadow of their cousins the East India Ducks, they still had a prominent place in Rotherhithe society. The reign of terror of the notorious Duck twins Ronnie and Reggie and their gang of ruthless drakes became too much for the authorities. From the public bar of their local "The Jolly Boatful of Gullible Tourists" spread a web of corruption. Resisting victims were lucky to escape with a good beaking.

The twins were arrested by Old Bill, convicted and sentenced by the local beak. Furiously quacking their innocence, their mother and family matriarch Mrs Mavis Duck fought in vain to restore the fortunes of her embattled clan. To no effect. A few years later, after a prolonged Duck Strike, they were privatised and became a marina for assorted overpriced and largely unused gin palaces.

Ameriducks

Duck Al Orange

Albert Duck of Orange came from one of the leading families in Europe. His great great uncle, William Prince of Orange, became King of England having closed his eyes and married Mary, confusing generations of British schoolchildren.

Europe had little to offer an ambitious duck on the periphery of a famous pond. He quit the Old World for the melting pot of the New. Arriving in Gold Rush California, he staked a productive claim, made oodles of dollars and invested them in citrus fruit cultivation.

As plain Al Orange, he gave his name to a County, became State Governor (ducks, actors, hey a donkey would do…) but enraged citizens, after yet another power failure, turned him into a gooey culinary platitude.

Emily Duckinson

The sort of poet who keeps university Eng Lit departments alive, her elliptical, if not obscure, verse has spawned thousands of studies, symposia and PhD theses. If she had not existed in 19th century Massachusetts, she would have been invented.

A mystic apprehension of the natural world and a preoccupation with fame, death and immortality suggest little by way of light banter around the Amherst dining table. The increasingly occasional guest was well advised to keep those carving knives safely out of reach.

Moby Duck

Voted 'Duck Most Likely to Succeed' by his fellow alumni of Canard College, Connecticut in 1963, Moby pursued his childhood fascination for magic into professional life. He specialised in large scale illusions. In the long hot summer of 1965 while swimming off the beach in Nantucket, he conceived the idea of swallowing his Uncle Jonah when next he fell from the family pedalo. He had never liked Uncle J, whose frequent inebriation meant that falls into the briny were plentiful that summer.

His demise was a fitting one for a duck who was happiest at the frontier of illusion and reality. Pursued by a myopic Yankee whaler improbably named Captain Ahab, Moby's despairing cry of "Dont shoot. I'm a duck" made matters worse. Ahab thought he was being warned that the Great White Whale was about to shoot at him so in best frontier style he beat the critter to the draw. Moby was filled with harpoons but took Ahab down with him.

Isadora Duckan

An exotic duck, she transformed the world of dance. No more ghastly gavottes or footling foxtrots. Isadora put the express into 'expressive' (or was it the excess into 'excessive' ?). She whirled about the stage, her webbed feet gyrating at warp speed, her wings describing random but complex patterns. The orderly disciplines of classical dance were abandoned with ..er..abandon.

Her sad end cautions us all (children). Do not climb into an open–topped Bugatti in Nice wearing a long scarf. As is well known, the scarf caught in the wheel of the car as it drove away. The scarf and Isadora had a brief tussle. The scarf won.

39

Euroducks

Terry Ducktyl

Easily dismissed as a sad old bird, Terence Ducktyl was, in his pomp, a fine feathery avian enforcer, swooping and soaring in milky primeval skies with his leathery chums. They cackled at their earthbound, huge but lumbering cousins − from a safe distance of course. Ah − life was good in the Dawn of Time. Lots of flesh to rip, nests to pillage, shaggy apes to chase.

Terence was undone by Vanity. An old story I fear. Vanity was an ambitious producer working for the BBC Wildlife Unit. Seduced by stardom, the front page of the Radio Times and an appearance on Parkinson ('which one is Parky ?' they all asked), Terence agreed to carry a camera into the skies. His erstwhile mates cast him out of the flock and he is now reduced to flapping mournfully around the Natural History Museum, with occasional background cameos in the 'Flying with Terry Ducktyls' series.

Jeanne Duck

Perhaps the greatest heroine of French medieval times, Jeanne inspired the dithering drakes of France to continue their long conflict with England. She had visions. Voices spoke to her. In these less enlightened times she would probably be sectioned under the Mental Health Act but the Spin Docteurs of the Ile de France (Rue Downing, Paris) could see the propaganda value of the Deluded Duck.

Sadly, she was captured by some rough English pheasants and cast loose by the Docteurs in Paris. She had the last cackle, however, achieving martyrdom, fame and crispness.

Ducktagnan

He grew up in an untidy pond, one of a lively brood born to proud but impoverished Gascon gentleducks. These somewhat shabby, rustic surroundings seemed an impossible setting for his vaunting, quacking, ambition. A much bigger pond beckoned. Paris itself !

The rutted tracks of 17th century France were enough to scramble the most enduring of eggs but Ducktagnan arrived in the capital city and waddled his way into the Kings Musqueducks – dashing, carefree young aristoducks who did not know the meaning of fear. Or personal hygiene.

With his famous companions Porduck, Athoduck and Araduck, Ducktagnan wielded a fearsome beak in the service of his King. Favourite targets were the Musqueducks of the Cardinal Duck de Richelieu. He survived novelists, film makers and chefs to become a Marshal of France with an assured place in The Pond of Fame.

47

The Duckesse of Malfi

The unfortunate eponymous heroine of a jolly play by John Webster, this theatrical 17th century aristoduck has a tough old life and a violent death. Imprisoned by her odious brothers because she had given birth to a commoner's child (oh the shame..), the play drips with blood, murder, revenge and lust. Just the thing to take Auntie Mabel to see on a wet Sunday afternoon.

Ferdinand
'My sister, O my sister ! there's the cause on't
Whether we fall by ambition, blood or lust
Like diamonds, we are cut with our own dust'   [*Dies*]

You get the general idea.

Le Mallard Imaginaire

A shadowy figure who achieved some celebrity in 17th century France for reasons that escape me. Anyway, Molière wrote a play about him so he must have been famous. This inventive duck was able to take the most outrageous liberties by persuading the gullible citizens of Paris that he was a figment of their imaginations. The adventures of his descendent, the almost legendary Scarlet Pimperduck, in Revolutionary times has been taken as a proof of something or other. Given the limitations of the medium, the recent film 'The Invisible Duck' is as faithful to Le Mallard as can be expected, with an unflinching performance in the main role by Gregory Peck.

Eider Orr

A notoriously indecisive duck from Denmark, Eider was usually to be found sitting on a fence. Unable to decide whether to be or not to be he found himself cast in an amateur production of Hamlet. It was only a waddle on part but at last Eider had found his vocation.

When the theatrical pendulum swung back towards the sorts of decisive roles for which he was ill suited, Eider was reduced to working in the duvet business. Salvation came with his discovery of politics. Umming and Ahhing was, he discovered, an essential attribute of the aspiring politiduck. His masterful balancing of factors and complete inability to take decisions proved irresistible. He had only to quack 'On the one wing ...' for his listeners to settle down in content. The rest is History.

Fyodor Mikhailovich Duckstoyevsky

This celebrated Muscovy duck was trained as a military engineer. Trenches, revetments, latrines. That kind of thing. No wonder he chose a somewhat different career. While hitchhiking from Omsk to Tomsk that summer, he was seized by the desire to write.

Recovering from gaming debts, he travelled in Europe. Travelling narrows the mind, contrary to popular belief. He returned an ardent Slavic Nationalist. He was both attracted and appalled by the churning inequalities of the Industrial Revolution as they afflicted Mother Russia. Readers are not advised to look for many laughs amidst the darkness.

He took his revenge on the world at large by writing extremely long novels as was the fashion of his age (see Charles Duckins). Exhausted readers managed the crime but couldn't take the punishment and baled out about page 356.

Il Duce

An Old English duck of advanced megalomanic character, Benedict Mousseline became as a young duck a village schoolmaster. The ducklings complained about his harsh discipline – the black uniforms, the saluting, the cold showers, the early morning marches around the pond. Miscreants were given a good beaking or dosed with castor oil. Their parents threw him out. Vowing revenge, he quit the village for the Larger Pond.

Benedict's methods became wildly popular (so long as you were doing the beaking and ladling out the castor oil). He rose to prominence. His jutting beak and ranting delivery went down a treat, especially with female ducks who often hurled their nether garments towards his podium. He became known simply as 'Il Duce'.

As always, Fate had the last chuckle. Benedict fell from power, was captured and executed by partisans. His body was suspended by the feet from a butchers hook with that of his mistress Clara Puddleduck.

Nonducks

'The Ducks' by Aristophanes

A recently discovered play by the old Greek dramatist, probably from his second period (425–406 BC). A chorus of ducks quacks at some length on the follies and foibles of mankind – a challenge for both the voice and makeup departments of modern theatres.

The current National Theatre production attempts to make the political allusions of the original relevant to the spin and superficiality of contemporary public life. Kenneth Branagh generally manages to keep a straight face in the leading role of Anitres but the audience is not sure whether to laugh or quack.

The Golden Duck

Many a village cricket scoreboard boasts a small duck amongst the numbers. For the sadly uninitiated, a batsperson who fails to score any runs at all when he or she bats is described as scoring a duck. This becomes golden if the person is out first ball.

An unknown and unfortunate duck, taking a quiet evening waddle around the village green one summer when cricket was in its infancy, chanced to be just beside the scorer when the opposing team's captain was dismissed without scoring. Untroubled but elated, he reached back without looking to his stack of numbers, not noticing that the unfortunate canard was passing at that precise moment. Quacking indignantly, the duck was seized and suspended from the scoreboard by the beak until close of play amid much rustic mirth.

S.D.A.S. (Sudden Duck Appearance Syndrome)

So there you are, walking along, minding your own business, when *suddenly* you are aware that you look like a duck ! Well, how distressing. But you are not alone. A Ducktor writes:

SDAS can affect any one at any time. No group in Society is immune. The only known cure is to sing Rule Britannia backwards three times (Ainnatirb Elur etc x 3) in a tuneless monotone. Stay calm. Hope the wind direction does not change. The most celebrated recent case is that of 'Duckface' in Three Weddings and a Funeral but that was probably a question of lighting, makeup and other cinematic arts.

North Duckota

Not to be confused with South Duckota. In a permanent euphoric if chilly state, this hardy North American duck rejoices in Bismark, Lake Sakakawea, a chunk of the upper Mississippi and a long-standing relationship with a Canada Goose.

In what purports to be Cockney rhyming slang (an invention of the English Tourist Board given an excruciating excursion by Duck van Dyke), a 'North and South' is a 'mouth'. Obviously a reference to the prominent beaks of the Duckota twins. As in 'what a marf, what a marf, what a Norf an Sarf, blimey wot a marf she got'. Excuse the cockney. Mate.

Mi Duck

Pronounced 'Mi Dook' in flat Derbyshire tones. Waddling down Green Lane in Derby towards Ranby's to purchase a tea towel, you may well be addressed in this way – a universal greeting in those stout and stolid parts. Any duck in fine feathers, regardless of age or circumstance, will be given this democratic tag.

Mildred Duck, now forgotten Patron Saint of Derbyshire, may be the origin of this Midland argot. Certainly her likeness enlivens the county crest although some macho heralds have substituted a Ram. There is something of Mildred's confident waddle in the swagger characteristic of the inhabitants of the county.

Note: Ranby's is now a pub – the original drapers of that name was taken over by Debenhams in the late 1960s.

Ducktility

n. The property of a material relating to its capacity to stretch before experiencing fracture:

1. *Ducks.* In Roman times, ducks found guilty of certain heinous crimes were attached by the neck to a horse travelling North and by the (webbed) feet to a horse travelling South. It kept the populus amused and became a frequent warm-up act before sanguinary gladiatorial contests. The ducktility of individual ducks was measured in seconds, depending on the speed of the horses. Obviously.

2. *Jokes.* The extent to which you may stretch a faintly amusing idea before tedium sets in for the reader. Measured in minutes but sometimes days. Hopefully.